HOW MANY PEOPLE TRAVELED THE OREGON TRAIL?

And Other Questions about the Trail West

Miriam Aronin

LERNER PUBLICATIONS COMPANY · MINNEAPOLIS

Copyright © 2012 by Lerner Publishing Group, Inc.

Lerner Publications Company
A division of Lerner Publishing Group, Inc.
241 First Avenue North
Minneapolis, MN 55401 U.S.A.

Website address: www.lernerbooks.com

Library of Congress Cataloging-in-Publication Data

Aronin, Miriam.
    How many people traveled the Oregon Trail? : and other questions about the
trail west / by Miriam Aronin.
        p.   cm. — (Six questions of American history)
    Includes bibliographical references and index.
    ISBN 978–0–7613–5332–4 (lib. bdg. : alk. paper)
        1. Oregon National Historic Trail—Juvenile literature. 2. Frontier and pioneer
life—West (U.S.)—Juvenile literature. 3. Overland journeys to the Pacific—Juvenile
literature. 4. West (U.S.)—History—19th century—Juvenile literature. 5. Oregon
Territory—History—Juvenile literature. I. Title.
    F597.A76 2012
    978'.02—dc23   2011022552

Manufactured in the United States of America
1 – DP – 12/31/11

TABLE OF CONTENTS 4

THE SIX
QUESTIONS
HELP YOU
DISCOVER THE
FACTS!

INTRODUCTION

Narcissa Prentiss and Marcus Whitman were married in New York on February 18, 1836. Narcissa began her married life by buying a pair of sturdy men's boots and sewing together a tent. She knew she would need them for her unusual honeymoon.

The newlyweds were not taking a short, fun vacation. Instead, they undertook an exhausting trek that would last months. To the Whitmans, the hard journey was worthwhile. They believed they had important work to do. They were traveling west to teach American Indians in Oregon about Christianity.

The Whitmans packed their belongings into a wagon. They joined a group that included fur trappers and traders. In May the group set out on the Oregon Trail. The journey held many dangers. The travelers could catch deadly diseases. They could run out of food. Or their wagons could break.

At that time, the United States and Great Britain shared control of Oregon Country. (This area included modern-day Oregon, Washington, Idaho, and part of Canada.) Just a few years after the Whitmans' trip, though, Americans began flocking to the area.

In the 1840s, the Oregon Trail would become the main route for these travelers. But how did the travelers know about this route? Who blazed the Oregon Trail?

Travelers packed everything in wagons like this one for the trip west.

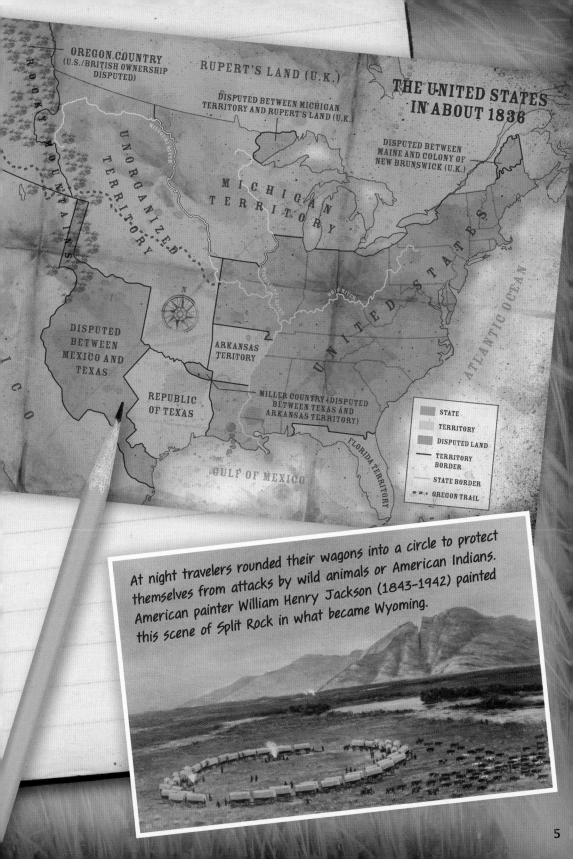

THE UNITED STATES IN ABOUT 1836

OREGON COUNTRY
(U.S./BRITISH OWNERSHIP DISPUTED)

RUPERT'S LAND (U.K.)

ROCKY MOUNTAINS

UNORGANIZED TERRITORY

MISSOURI RIVER

DISPUTED BETWEEN MICHIGAN TERRITORY AND RUPERT'S LAND (U.K.)

DISPUTED BETWEEN MAINE AND COLONY OF NEW BRUNSWICK (U.K.)

MICHIGAN TERRITORY

N

MISSISSIPPI RIVER

OHIO RIVER

UNITED STATES

ATLANTIC OCEAN

MEXICO

DISPUTED BETWEEN MEXICO AND TEXAS

ARKANSAS TERRITORY

REPUBLIC OF TEXAS

MILLER COUNTRY (DISPUTED BETWEEN TEXAS AND ARKANSAS TERRITORY)

FLORIDA TERRITORY

GULF OF MEXICO

STATE
TERRITORY
DISPUTED LAND
TERRITORY BORDER
STATE BORDER
OREGON TRAIL

At night travelers rounded their wagons into a circle to protect themselves from attacks by wild animals or American Indians. American painter William Henry Jackson (1843–1942) painted this scene of Split Rock in what became Wyoming.

American Indian Sacagawea interprets for Meriwether Lewis and William Clark during a meeting with the Chinook Indians of the Pacific Northwest. American artist Charles Russell painted this image in 1805.

ONE TRAILBLAZERS

The first people to live in modern-day Oregon were American Indians. Then, in the 1500s, Spanish explorers sailed their ships to the area, but they did not stay long.

More than two hundred years later, U.S. president Thomas Jefferson sent an expedition to explore the land west of the Mississippi River. The explorers, led by Meriwether Lewis and William Clark, reached Oregon in 1805.

When they returned, Lewis and Clark wrote reports about what they had seen. They said that the land in Oregon Country was rich and beautiful. It had many

expedition

a group making a journey for a particular reason

beavers and otters, animals hunted for their warm furs. Clark especially admired the animal skins that American Indians in Oregon wore. He wrote that they were "more beautiful than any fur I had ever Seen."

That interested New York businessman John Jacob Astor. Astor thought he could make money buying and selling these furs. In 1810 he sent men to set up a trading post in Oregon. The fur traders named their new trading post after their boss. Fort Astor, or Astoria, became the first American settlement in Oregon Country.

WHO WAS JOHN JACOB ASTOR?

John Jacob Astor was an important American businessman. By the early 1800s, he had become rich trading furs. Astor later bought buildings and land in New York City. Members of the wealthy Astor family used their money to help people in New York throughout the 1800s. The Astors even helped to found the city's main public library.

John Jacob Astor

Astoria did not get off to a promising start. Soon after they arrived, a group of the traders sailed up the Columbia River. On their trip, the ship's captain started a fight with local American Indians. Most of the traders were killed in the fight. Only one man escaped. He brought the sad news back to Astoria. The men there knew they had to tell their boss the sad news. But John Jacob Astor lived in New York, thousands of miles away.

The traders decided to send a small group of men back east with the message. They chose twenty-seven-year-old Robert Stuart to lead the group. Stuart and his men started out in June 1812 in canoes and then continued on horseback. They had no road to follow, so they traveled slowly. In September Crow Indians stole their horses. Soon it would be winter. Could the travelers cross the steep Rocky Mountains on foot?

Luckily, Stuart found a flat route where the men could pass through safely. This narrow plain crossed the mountains at about 7,000 feet (2,134 meters) above sea level. But the travelers were still far from their destination. They walked all winter. On April 30, 1813, they finally reached Saint Louis, Missouri. From there, Stuart could ride to New York to deliver his message.

plain: a large, level area without trees

sea level: the height of the top of the sea or ocean. Sea level is used as the starting point to measure the height of landforms such as mountains.

Many men, women, and children would soon follow the traders' path west. But this group was going east. Robert Stuart had blazed the Oregon Trail backward!

WHAT WERE THE BRITISH DOING IN OREGON?

John Jacob Astor was not the only one who was interested in Oregon's furs. So were British traders. That's why the British had their eye on Astoria. Once war broke out, they were quick to claim Oregon Country—and its furs. After the war, the British Hudson's Bay Company (HBC) controlled much of Oregon's fur trade. John McLoughlin worked for the company from 1821 to 1846. Besides trading furs, he also welcomed many travelers into his home as guests. He even helped U.S. settlers who were moving to Oregon. HBC still exists as a company. It is no longer in the fur-trading business, though.

While Stuart and his men were traveling, the United States and Great Britain had gone to war— the War of 1812 (1812–1815). In 1813 British forces captured Astoria. The following year, the warring countries signed a peace treaty. They later promised to share control of Oregon Country.

NEXT QUESTION

WHY DID AMERICANS BEGIN GOING WEST?

Jedediah Smith survived a bear attack in 1824. Exploring the western United States brought many dangers.

TWO RETURN TO SOUTH PASS

Americans had been so busy with the War of 1812 that they paid little attention to Robert Stuart's new route. But not everyone had lost interest in the furs found in the West.

In 1822 twenty-three-year-old Jedediah Smith joined a trading expedition to the Upper Missouri River. The next year, while Smith was leading a group of traders, Crow Indians told him about the rich furs west of the Rocky Mountains. They even told him the best way to reach those furs—over a high plain through the Rockies. This was the same path Robert Stuart had taken. Americans later called it South Pass because it was south of Lewis and Clark's route. It was easier than Lewis and Clark's route too!

Jedediah Smith's search for furs took him to Oregon and California. To get there, he crossed South Pass several times. He quickly became an expert about traveling and trading in the West. Soon he took over the fur-trading business.

WHO WAS JEDEDIAH SMITH?

Jedediah Smith was an expert hunter and trader who lived in the American wilderness. "I started into the mountains with the determination of becoming a first-rate hunter," he wrote, "of making myself thoroughly acquainted with the character and habits of the Indians, of tracing out the sources of the Columbia River, and following it to its mouth and of making the whole profitable to me." Smith spent much of the 1820s in the wilderness. He opened up new routes to California and Oregon. He even became part owner of a successful trading business. Within a few years, he met all of his goals.

Jedediah Smith

During the evenings, travelers sat around campfires, played music, and exchanged stories, resting up for the next day.

In the 1820s, almost all the travelers on the early Oregon Trail were traders and mountain men like Jedediah Smith. That was about to change. In 1830 Smith's business partner, William Sublette, organized a group of ten wagons to travel together through South Pass. This became the first wagon train to make it through the Rockies.

Three years after Sublette's wagon train crossed South Pass, a letter appeared in a New York Christian newspaper. According to the letter, Nez Percé Indians were asking questions about the "white man's Book of Heaven."

U.S. Christians were happy that the Nez Percé were interested in the Bible. Church leaders hoped the Nez Percé and members of other American Indian groups would become Christians too. Churches began sending missionaries west to teach about Christianity.

One of those missionaries was Dr. Marcus Whitman from New York. Whitman first went to Oregon in 1835. The next year, he returned east and married Narcissa Prentiss. The two set out right away for Oregon to keep working as missionaries.

A Christian missionary preaches to American Indians and fur traders in the American West.

In the beginning, the journey was exciting. Narcissa liked having meals picnic-style on a blanket on the ground. Sometimes the travelers ate buffalo meat three meals a day. She enjoyed that too. "I never was so contented and happy before," she wrote in her journal.

Soon, though, the way became more difficult. The Whitmans and their group climbed steep mountains. They crossed countless rivers and streams. No matter how tired they became, they kept traveling.

Pioneers had to endure the hard journey through the Rocky Mountains. They struggled up steep mountainsides and through blinding snowstorms.

As they grew close to the end of their trip, the path became too rough for wagons. The Whitmans had to leave behind whatever their pack animals could not carry.

At last, the newlyweds reached Oregon. They set up their mission at Waiilatpu. For the next ten years, the Whitman Mission would be an important landmark. It signaled to travelers that they had nearly arrived at their destination.

In 1930 William Henry Jackson painted this scene of the Marcus and Narcissa Whitman Mission in Oregon.

15

HOW DID ARTISTS AND WRITERS DEPICT THE OREGON TRAIL?

Like Jason Lee, artists and writers fed Americans' dreams of the West. In 1837 painter Alfred Jacob Miller followed the Oregon Trail as far as the Rocky Mountains. On the way, he made sketches of what he saw. Miller later turned these sketches into thrilling paintings of American Indians, landscapes, and trail landmarks. The famous writer Washington Irving also published *The Adventures of Captain Bonneville* in 1837. This exciting book told the true story of an army officer's travels on trails through the West.

Another missionary named Jason Lee also traveled to Oregon in the 1830s. Besides teaching American Indians, he was interested in bringing more U.S. Christians to settle in Oregon.

In 1838 Lee went back east and began making speeches.

American artist Alfred Jacob Miller was inspired to paint the people and sights he saw along the Oregon Trail. In this scene, Oglala Lakota camp on the outskirts of Fort Laramie in Wyoming.

Missionary Jason Lee went to Oregon to spread the teachings of Christianity to American Indians. He later encouraged Christians from the East Coast to settle in the West.

He encouraged Americans to move west. He spoke about Oregon's rich farmland. He talked about driving out the British and making Oregon Country the property of the United States.

As Americans learned more about the area, many caught "Oregon fever." They dreamed about a better life in the far West.

NEXT QUESTION

WHERE DID PEOPLE BEGIN THEIR JOURNEY ON THE OREGON TRAIL?

This engraving by Hermann Meyer shows the streets and courthouse of Independence, Missouri, in 1850. Independence was a jumping-off point for travelers leaving for the West.

THREE TRAVELERS JUMP OFF

In 1842 the Whitmans received a message from their church group. The group wanted to stop supporting its missions in Oregon. That winter Marcus Whitman returned to the East. He persuaded the group to change its plan. In spring 1843, he prepared to return to Oregon with the good news.

When he reached Independence, Missouri, a surprise was waiting for him. Almost one thousand emigrants were preparing to leave on the Oregon Trail!

emigrants | people who leave one place to move to another

Emigrants "jumped off," or began their journey, at the Missouri River. Many started in Independence. Some jumped off from other towns such as Saint Joseph,

Missouri, and Council Bluffs, Iowa. Most pioneers traveled to their jumping-off points by steamboat. When they arrived, they needed two or three weeks to buy supplies and prepare for their trip.

Many families sold all their possessions to pay for supplies for the journey. The first thing emigrants needed was a wagon. It had to be light enough to not wear out the animals that pulled it. It had to be large enough to carry supplies for the long journey. But it also had to be small enough to get through narrow mountain trails and tricky river crossings. Finally, it had to be sturdy enough to provide shelter.

A drawing by William Henry Jackson shows wagons, livestock, horses, and people making the dusty journey along the Oregon Trail. This landmark, known as Devil's Gate, is along the Sweetwater River in Wyoming.

a type of covered wagon used on the Oregon Trail

One popular kind of wagon was called a prairie schooner. Its light-colored cover reminded people of the sails of a schooner, a kind of ship. A prairie schooner could carry around 1,000 to 1,500 pounds (454 to 680 kilograms) of supplies. It was about 4 feet (1.2 m) wide and 10 to 12 feet (3 to 3.7 m) long. In this small space, early emigrants had to fit everything they needed for their journey and their life in Oregon.

The most important supplies were food for the months of travel. An emigrant family would need several hundred pounds of flour and several hundred more of bacon. They also packed sugar, salt, coffee, dried fruit, and other dry foods.

Every family needed a heavy cooking pot and pan, sturdy tin dishes, and weapons. Guns were used for hunting or defense in case of meetings with unfriendly American Indians.

The inside of a prairie schooner was crammed with a family's possessions. They might include furniture, a spinning wheel, silverware, pots and pans, and more.

WHY OXEN?

Emigrants had to choose which kinds of animals would pull their wagons on the Oregon Trail. Horses were fast but not strong enough for the long journey. Horses also made tempting targets for thieves. Even worse, horses often became sick from eating tough prairie grass and drinking bad water along the trail. Mules were sturdier but hard to control. They sometimes panicked and drowned when crossing rivers. Also, emigrants needed eight to ten mules to have enough strength to pull a loaded wagon.

Oxen traveled at only 2 miles (3.2 km) per hour. But they were stronger than mules or horses. They would make good farmworkers when they got to Oregon. Most emigrants harnessed their wagons to four or six oxen.

Most emigrants brought along basic farm equipment, such as a plow, to use in Oregon. A heavy cotton canvas cover kept the goods in the wagon out of the wind, dust, and rain.

Oxen or mules pulled the bumpy wagons stuffed full of supplies along the trail. Little space was left for people to ride inside. Instead, almost everyone walked. Their 2,000-mile (3,219 km) journey would take between four and six months.

> large male cattle that can pull heavy loads

When the first large group of emigrants was ready to go, Dr. Whitman joined the gigantic wagon train. The pioneers were glad to have such an experienced traveler as their guide.

NEXT QUESTION

WHAT WAS LIFE LIKE ON THE OREGON TRAIL?

River crossings were tricky. Emigrants had to get their livestock and belongings across the river safely.

FOUR FOLLOWING THE TRAIL

After emigrants jumped off, they followed the first part of the Oregon Trail through flat plains. The ground became rougher as travelers followed the Platte River west. This was one of the first rivers the emigrants had to cross.

Crossing a river was not easy. Wagons had to be made waterproof and then dragged or floated to the other side. Once many people had started traveling west, travelers could pay for a ferry to carry their wagons across some rivers.

a boat or raft that carries goods or people over water

On the trail, emigrants woke up and ate breakfast before dawn. By seven o'clock, the wagon train was moving. Except for a short lunch break, they continued traveling until almost sunset. In that time, they traveled about 15 miles (24 km). Then they made camp and ate dinner. For a short time, they might sing, play music, dance, or play cards. Bedtime came early so the travelers could rest before their next long day.

THE OREGON TRAIL

This map shows the route of the Oregon Trail, from Independence, Missouri, west through the Rocky Mountains.

---- OREGON TRAIL
—— CURRENT STATE BORDER

At night, men took turns keeping guard. Almost every man was armed with a gun. The emigrants feared American Indian attacks. However, most Indians were interested in trading, not in causing harm.

As they traveled, emigrants looked for the famous landmarks along the way. One landmark, Courthouse Rock, looked like a castle. This gigantic rock formation could be seen from 40 miles (64 km) away. For the emigrants, that was about a three-day journey.

LANDMARKS
Travelers looked for Jail Rock, Courthouse Rock, and Chimney Rock as they crossed what became Nebraska on their way west.

NEBRASKA

to Fort Laramie (60 miles/ 97 km)

Scottsbluff

Mormon Pioneer Trail

Oregon Trail

North Platte River

CHIMNEY ROCK NATIONAL HISTORIC SITE

COURTHOUSE ROCK

JAIL ROCK

Bridgeport

GPS

Courthouse Rock *(left)* and Jail Rock *(right)* were two of the landmarks travelers looked for along the Oregon Trail.

Fort Laramie was a welcome sight for travelers after crossing the plains. They could rest before tackling the difficult journey farther west. Famed American artist Frederic Remington (1861–1909) created this print.

After traveling more than 600 miles (966 km), pioneers reached Fort Laramie, a trading post in what became Wyoming. There, travelers rested and repaired their wagons. If they had enough money, they could also buy more supplies.

Most emigrants could not afford extra supplies. Instead, they became experts at using whatever they found on the trail. The travelers often hunted buffalo and other animals for food and fuel. Emigrants often ran out of wood for their campfires. Then they used dried buffalo droppings, called buffalo chips, instead.

HOW DID EMIGRANTS GET ALONG ON THE TRAIL?

Most wagon trains chose a captain to act as their leader. Travelers also wrote rules about how to behave, solve disagreements, and punish crimes. Rules even covered the order of the wagons on the trail. All the rolling wagons kicked up a lot of dust. That made traveling at the end of the train uncomfortable. Many groups agreed to have the wagons change places every day. That way, everyone had a turn in the front of the line, where it was less dusty.

Of all the landmarks on the Oregon Trail, Independence Rock is one of the most famous. Emigrants who reached the huge, turtle-shaped rock by July 4 were making good time. They were likely to arrive at their destination before winter weather made travel very risky.

A wagon train passes Independence Rock in Wyoming. This painting was created by William Henry Jackson in 1865.

This wagon train continues westward after crossing the Rocky Mountains.

The emigrants slowly climbed into the Rocky Mountains. At South Pass, they crossed the Continental Divide. Still, the exhausted emigrants were less than halfway to their destination.

The farther they traveled, the harder the way became. Flat plains gave way to hills and mountains. There were more rivers to cross. Dust and insects plagued the travelers. The emigrants walked through blazing sun and pouring rain. Their oxen became thin and weak from constantly pulling heavy wagons.

an imaginary line across the mountains in Canada, the United States, Central America, and South America that marks where water on one side flows west to the Pacific Ocean and water on the other side flows east to the Atlantic Ocean

About one in ten travelers did not survive the hardships of the trail. Deadly diseases such as cholera could spread quickly through a wagon train. Many people also suffered injuries and death from terrible accidents.

The sad story of the Sager family shows some of the dangers emigrants faced. Catherine Sager was traveling with her parents and six brothers and sisters. On August 1, 1844,

WHAT HAPPENED TO THE DONNER PARTY?

The journey west was long and tiring. Some people were tempted to take shortcuts, or cutoffs, to save time. These unmarked routes could be dangerous. In 1846 the Donner and Reed families followed a cutoff. The way was rough, though, and they had to travel slowly. In October they reached the mountains of California's Sierra Nevada. Then heavy snow began to fall.

The emigrants were trapped. They had little food. Their animals quickly froze or starved. Their wagons were buried under 40-foot (12 m) snowdrifts. When rescuers arrived in February, forty-one of the eighty-seven travelers had died. Those still alive were starving. To survive, they had been forced to eat the bodies of the dead.

This memorial statue in California is dedicated to members of the Donner Party.

VIRILE TO RISK AND FIND; KINDLY WITHAL AND A READY HELP. FACING THE BRUNT OF FATE INDOMI- TABLE.— UNAFRAID.

These stones outline the graves of two emigrants who died along the Oregon Trail. Accidents and sickness caused many of the deaths along the trail west.

Catherine tried to climb onto a moving wagon. Then, she recalled later, "My dress caught . . . and I was thrown under the wagon wheel." The wheel crushed and badly broke one of her legs. Fortunately, Catherine survived.

Her parents were not as lucky. Soon after Catherine's injury, her father became ill and died. Before long, her mother caught a terrible disease called camp fever. Soon Mrs. Sager too was dead.

camp fever: a form of typhus, a disease that causes high fever, chills, rashes, and confusion

NEXT QUESTION

WHERE DID THE EMIGRANTS SETTLE?

This illustration, made in 1853, shows members of the Church of Latter-Day Saints leaving Illinois for Utah. They sought religious freedom in the West.

FIVE NEW HOMES

No matter what happened, the wagons rolled on toward Oregon. The determined pioneers walked alongside.

After the Sagers' parents died, other members of their wagon train helped the seven young orphans. When the group reached Waiilatpu, the Whitmans adopted the children. The other emigrants continued on. They made their new homes in the fertile farm country of Oregon's Willamette River valley.

able to produce large amounts of plants such as farm crops

Not all the travelers on the Oregon Trail were headed for Oregon, though. Mormons, or members of the Church of Latter-Day Saints, had a different destination in mind.

The Mormons had already tried to settle in New York, Ohio, Missouri, and Illinois. In each place, they faced persecution for their religious beliefs. Mormon beliefs at that time included allowing a man to marry more than one woman. Others especially disapproved of this practice. Finally, in 1844, the church's founder, Joseph Smith, was murdered in Nauvoo, Illinois.

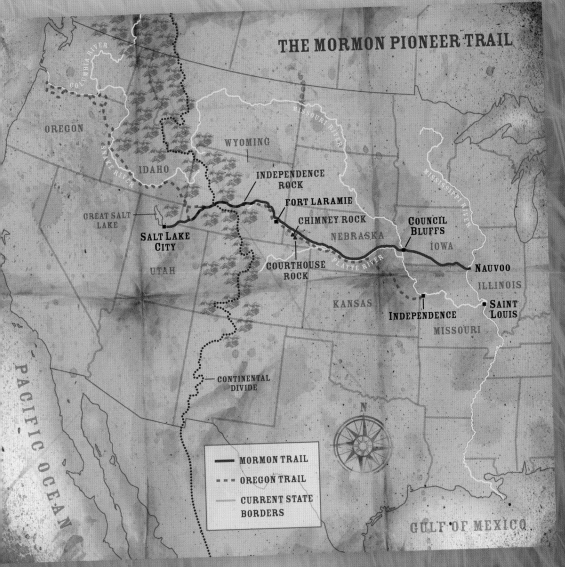

THE MORMON PIONEER TRAIL

OREGON

WYOMING

IDAHO

INDEPENDENCE ROCK

FORT LARAMIE

CHIMNEY ROCK

GREAT SALT LAKE

SALT LAKE CITY

NEBRASKA

COUNCIL BLUFFS

IOWA

UTAH

COURTHOUSE ROCK

PLATTE RIVER

NAUVOO

ILLINOIS

KANSAS

INDEPENDENCE

SAINT LOUIS

MISSOURI

CONTINENTAL DIVIDE

N

PACIFIC OCEAN

MORMON TRAIL
OREGON TRAIL
CURRENT STATE BORDERS

GULF OF MEXICO

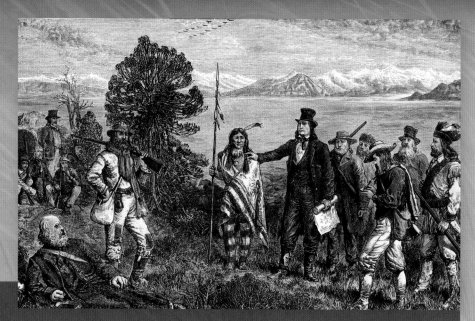

Mormon leader Brigham Young *(in black hat)* and his followers arrived in Utah in 1847. The Mormons settled on the shores of the Great Salt Lake. Their community would become Utah's capital, Salt Lake City.

Brigham Young, the new Mormon leader, had seen enough. He decided to take his people west, to an area where they would be safe. Young wanted a place where few other settlers would bother them. He led the first group of Mormon travelers to modern-day Utah in 1847. When they reached the valley of the Great Salt Lake, he knew he had found the right spot. Young believed it was God's will that the Mormons should settle there.

More and more Mormons poured into the area over the coming years. Many were too poor to buy wagons and animals. Instead, they pushed their belongings in wheeled handcarts along the Oregon Trail.

When the Mormons began moving to Utah, the area belonged to Mexico. But the United States and Mexico were at war. When the war ended in 1848, the United States gained control of much of the Southwest. The new American lands included Utah and California. The United States gained even more new land two years earlier. That's when the British had given up control of all of Oregon Country south of [latitude] 49° north, including the present-day states of Oregon and Washington. Many settlers in these new areas wanted to take part in the U.S. government. In 1848 lawmakers set up the first official U.S. government in the far West— Oregon Territory.

> **latitude** a distance north or south of the equator, measured from 0 to 90 degrees

Statue of Dr. Marcus Whitman

WHAT HAPPENED TO THE WHITMAN MISSION?

In 1847 a terrible disease called measles swept through the Waiilatpu area. Dr. Whitman treated everyone who became ill. Most white children survived, because their bodies had immunity, or a natural resistance, to the disease. Sadly, Cayuse Indians had little immunity to measles.

When most of the Cayuse patients died, the Cayuse people blamed the doctor. On November 29, a group of angry Cayuse swept into the mission to take revenge. At least fourteen people were killed, including Marcus and Narcissa Whitman. The news of the tragedy helped convince lawmakers in Washington, D.C., that Oregon needed a new government to protect its citizens.

THE POWER OF MANIFEST DESTINY

The Mexican-American War (1846–1848) was all about land—Utah, New Mexico, Wyoming, Nevada, Texas, and California. Many Americans in the 1840s believed the United States should stretch all the way between the Atlantic and Pacific oceans. In 1845 one magazine article expressed this feeling with the phrase "manifest destiny." That meant that expanding the United States to the west was clearly God's plan.

Belief in manifest destiny inspired many settlers to move west. They felt they were taking part in a great patriotic mission. Manifest destiny also helped persuade the U.S. government to go to war with Mexico for the western lands.

That same year, gold was discovered at Sutter's Mill in California. By 1849 "forty-niners" were rushing to California to search for their own gold. Some traveled by boat. About twenty thousand more took the Oregon Trail.

California's exploding population put it on the fast track for U.S. statehood. In 1849 it asked to join the Union. There was just one problem. California wanted to become a free state—a state that would not allow slavery.

This 1872 painting by John Gast is named *American Progress*. The female figure represents white Americans bringing farming, industry, and transportation to the Wild West. This, however, meant forcing American Indians from their homes and disrupting lives.

This group of gold miners was photographed in Taylorsville, California, in 1849. In that year, thousands of people seeking their fortunes traveled west in the great California gold rush.

But supporters of slavery did not like this plan. At last, supporters and opponents of slavery came to an agreement. The Compromise of 1850 allowed California to become a free state. The agreement also set up Utah Territory. The territory's citizens would decide whether to allow slavery there. Over the next few years, tens of thousands of gold rush settlers poured into the Union's newest state. Many came partway on the Oregon Trail.

a settlement to a disagreement in which each side agrees to give up some of the things it wants

NEXT QUESTION

WHEN DID PEOPLE STOP TRAVELING ON THE OREGON TRAIL?

In 1900 Frederic Remington painted this image of a Pony Express rider changing horses. The entire Pony Express route was about 1,900 miles (3,058 km) long.

SIX THE END OF THE TRAIL

By 1850 Oregon Territory, Utah Territory, and the state of California were part of the United States. As new settlers built homes, governments, and businesses, they often needed to send messages quickly between the East and the West.

In 1860 three businessmen started the Pony Express to do just that. The owners hired speedy riders to carry mail on horseback between Saint Joseph, Missouri, and Sacramento, California. For much of the way, the riders followed the Oregon Trail. To keep up their speed, they stopped to change horses every 15 miles (24 km). Pony

Express riders could complete their journey in just ten days.

Despite its fast riders, the Pony Express lasted less than two years. In 1861 the Western Union company set up a much quicker way to send messages over long distances. It built a telegraph line from the East to Salt Lake City. Then it connected that line to other companies' lines to San Francisco, California. Suddenly people could send urgent messages across the country almost instantly. With the telegraph, the Pony Express was no longer needed. New technology was beginning to take the place of the Oregon Trail.

telegraph
system of sending coded messages over electric wires

HOW DID THE TELEGRAPH WORK?

Before telephones were invented, people used telegraph machines to send urgent news over long distances. Using electric wires, telegraph machines could transmit messages from place to place almost instantly. First, an operator on the sending end tapped out a message on one key. When the key was pressed, electricity flowed through the wire. The operator on the other end heard a clicking sound. When the key was lifted, the electric flow and the clicking stopped. Telegraph operators sent messages using a code made up of short and long clicks. Each set of clicks represented one letter. As the operator on the receiving end of the wire listened to the clicks, he or she decoded them and wrote out the final message.

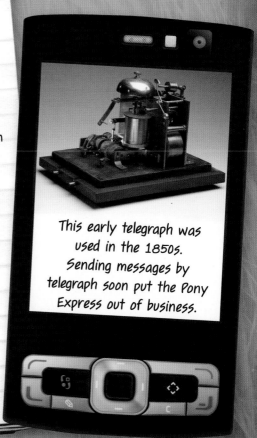

This early telegraph was used in the 1850s. Sending messages by telegraph soon put the Pony Express out of business.

going all the way across a continent, such as North America

Eight years after the telegraph arrived, another new technology brought big changes to the West. In 1869 workers finished the Transcontinental Railroad. Its tracks stretched all the way across North America from east to west. The western branch of the railroad ran from Sacramento, California, to Omaha, Nebraska.

The new train route was a much faster and easier way to travel than the Oregon Trail. Instead of spending months walking on rough ground, travelers who started in Omaha rode comfortably to the western coast in less than a week.

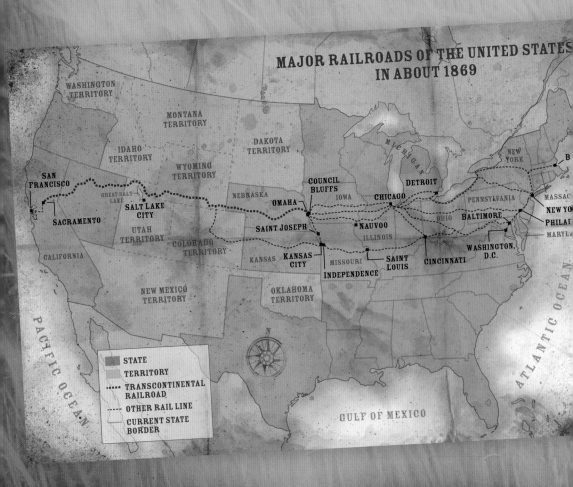

MAJOR RAILROADS OF THE UNITED STATES
IN ABOUT 1869

STATE
TERRITORY
TRANSCONTINENTAL RAILROAD
OTHER RAIL LINE
CURRENT STATE BORDER

WHERE WAS THE TRANSCONTINENTAL RAILROAD COMPLETED?

The Transcontinental Railroad was made from two different sets of tracks. In 1862 workers in Sacramento, California, began building tracks going east for the Central Pacific Railroad. Meanwhile, workers in Omaha, Nebraska, started building the Union Pacific Railroad's tracks heading west. The tracks met in Promontory, Utah, in May 1869. To celebrate, one wealthy San Francisco builder had a large railroad spike made out of pure gold. On one side, he had these words carved: "May God continue the unity of our country as the railroad unites the two great Oceans of the world."

After taking the train to California, those headed for Oregon could take a fairly short wagon trip to complete their journey.

Not everyone could afford train tickets. Still, in the 1870s and the 1880s, fewer and fewer emigrants followed the wagon tracks of the Oregon Trail west.

On May 10, 1869, the last spike was driven into the tracks of the first Transcontinental Railroad.

By 1906 between two hundred thousand and five hundred thousand people had taken the Oregon Trail west. But almost no one was still traveling on the trail. Seventy-five-year-old Ezra Meeker worried that Americans would forget this important part of their history. He came up with a daring plan.

When he was just twenty-one years old, Meeker had traveled from Iowa to Oregon with his wife and their newborn baby. More than fifty years later, he decided to return east the same way he had come. He packed his supplies in a wagon pulled by a team of two oxen.

This time, he traveled alone. On his way, he stopped to make speeches about the importance of the Oregon Trail. He set up markers in places where the trail had passed.

Meeker's journey and the book he wrote about his experiences impressed many Americans—including President Theodore Roosevelt.

Ezra Meeker

On Oregon Trail

Ezra Meeker near Bellevue

In about 1910, a photographer captured Ezra Meeker on his journey along the Oregon Trail. Here he is pictured near Bellevue, Nebraska.

After meeting Meeker, President Roosevelt promised to give money to help preserve the historic trail.

In 1910 Meeker made the overland journey one last time. Five years later, he crossed the trail in an early airplane. His travels taught Americans about the Oregon Trail. He helped make sure that this important part of our country's history would never be forgotten.

NEXT QUESTION

HOW DO WE KNOW ABOUT THE EXPERIENCES OF TRAVELERS ON THE OREGON TRAIL?

Primary Source: The Diary of Narcissa Whitman

Much of what we know about the Oregon Trail comes from the travelers themselves. Historians estimate that as many as three thousand travelers on the trail wrote about their experiences in diaries or journals. That's about one out of every two hundred emigrants!

A primary source is a document written by a person who was alive at the time of an event. It is often a firsthand description of something that happened in history. Letters, journals, and newspaper articles are examples of primary sources. The following primary source is from Narcissa Whitman's diary. It describes some of the hardships of traveling on the Oregon Trail.

> 25th [of July 1836].—Came fifteen miles [24 km] to-day; encamped on Smith's creek, a small branch of Bear creek. The ride has been very mountainous—paths winding on the sides of steep mountains. In some places the path is so narrow as scarcely to afford room for the animal to place his foot. One after another we pass along with cautious step. . . .
> Husband [Marcus Whitman] has had a tedious time with the wagon to-day. It got stuck in the creek this morning when crossing, and he was obliged to wade considerably in getting it out. After that, in going between the mountains, on the side of one . . . the wagon was upset twice; it was a greater wonder that it was not turning somersaults continually.

TELL YOUR OREGON TRAIL STORY

Imagine you are an emigrant traveling on the Oregon Trail. You hope to start a new life in the West. To get there, though, you have to spend months traveling there by foot and wagon. Write a journal entry or a letter to a friend back east describing your experiences.

WHERE are you originally from?

WHERE are you going? (Are you headed for Oregon, California, Utah, or somewhere else?)

WHY are you going to the West?

WHEN did you begin the journey?

WHAT sights have you seen along the trail?

WHO else is in your wagon train?

HOW do you get along with the other travelers?

USE **WHO, WHAT, WHERE WHY, WHEN,** AND **HOW** TO THINK OF OTHER QUESTIONS TO HELP YOU CREATE YOUR STORY!

Timeline

1805

The Lewis and Clark expedition arrives in Oregon Country.

1811

John Jacob Astor's men set up a fur-trading post at Astoria.

1812–1813

Robert Stuart blazes the Oregon Trail.

1813

British forces take over Astoria.

1822

Jedediah Smith heads west on a fur-trading expedition.

1830

William Sublette brings the first wagon train over the Rocky Mountains.

1836

Marcus and Narcissa Whitman travel over the Oregon Trail to settle in Oregon. Narcissa and Eliza Spalding, another missionary's wife, are the first white women to follow the trail west.

1837

Washington Irving publishes *The Adventures of Captain Bonneville*. Alfred Jacob Miller uses the Oregon Trail as inspiration for his paintings.

1838

Missionary Jason Lee urges U.S. Christians to move west.

1843

A wagon train of about one thousand emigrants heads west. (This huge wagon train is sometimes called the Great Migration.)

1846

The United States and Great Britain agree to split Oregon Country at latitude 49° north. Everything north of that line will belong to the British. Everything south of it will belong to the United States.

1847

Brigham Young leads the first group of **Mormons** to the Great Salt Lake valley.

Marcus and Narcissa Whitman and others at the Whitman Mission are murdered.

1848

The United States wins the Mexican-American War.

Oregon becomes a U.S. territory.

Gold is discovered at Sutter's Mill in California.

1849

The California gold rush begins. Thousands of forty-niners head west in search of gold.

1850

Under the Compromise of 1850, California becomes a state, and Utah becomes a U.S. territory.

1869

The Transcontinental Railroad is finished. Passengers can ride from Omaha, Nebraska, to Sacramento, California.

1906

Ezra Meeker takes the Oregon Trail east by wagon.

Source Notes

7 Meriwether Lewis and William Clark, *The Journals of Lewis and Clark*, Journal of William Clark, November 20, 1805 (1804–1806; Project Gutenberg, 2005), http://www.gutenberg.org/cache/epub/8419/pg8419.html (August 10, 2011).

11 Stephen W. Sears, "Trail Blazer of the Far West," *American Heritage Magazine*, 1963, 2011, http://www.americanheritage.com/content/trail-blazer-far-west (August 10, 2011).

12 David Dary, *The Oregon Trail: An American Saga* (New York: Alfred A. Knopf, 2004), 56.

14 Narcissa Whitman, "Diaries and Journals of Narcissa Whitman 1836," The Oregon Trail, n.d., http://www.isu.edu/~trinmich/00.ar.whitman1.html (August 10, 2011).

29 Catherine Sager Pringle, "Across the Plains in 1844," *The Oregon Trail*, 2011, http://www.isu.edu/~trinmich/00.ar.sager1.html (August 10, 2011).

39 National Park Service, "Golden Spike," NPS, n.d., http://www.nps.gov/gosp/historyculture/upload/Spikes.pdf (August 10, 2011).

42 Whitman, "Diaries and Journals."

Selected Bibliography

American Heritage, eds. *Westward on the Oregon Trail*. New York: American Heritage Publishing, 1962.

Dary, David. *The Oregon Trail: An American Saga*. New York: Alfred A. Knopf, 2004.

McCartney, Laton. *Across the Great Divide: Robert Stuart and the Discovery of the Oregon Trail*. New York: Free Press, 2003.

Parkman, Francis. *The Oregon Trail; The Conspiracy of Pontiac*. New York: Library of America, 1991.

Ridge, Martin, ed. *Westward Journeys: Memoirs of Jesse A. Applegate and Lavinia Honeyman Porter Who Traveled the Oregon Trail*. Chicago: R. R. Donnelly and Sons, 1989.

Whitman, Narcissa. "Diaries and Journals of Narcissa Whitman 1836." The Oregon Trail. N.d. http://www.isu.edu/~trinmich/00.ar.whitman1.html (August 10, 2011).

Further Reading and Websites

Brill, Marlene Targ. *The Rough-Riding Adventure of Bronco Charlie, Pony Express Rider*. Minneapolis: Graphic Universe, 2011. Young Bronco Charlie dreams of being a Pony Express rider. In this graphic novel, he gets a chance to prove he's ready.

Figley, Marty Rhodes. *Clara Morgan and the Oregon Trail Journey*. Minneapolis: Millbrook Press, 2011. Read the story of an eleven-year-old girl traveling on the Oregon Trail with her family. Then perform the story as a Reader's Theater play!

Friedman, Mel. *The Oregon Trail*. New York: Children's Press, 2010. Learn facts and trivia about the explorers and pioneers who traveled on the Oregon Trail.

Harness, Cheryl. *The Tragic Tale of Narcissa Whitman and a Faithful History of the Oregon Trail*. Washington, DC: National Geographic, 2006. Follow the whole story of Narcissa Whitman's life and her exciting trip west on the Oregon Trail.

Historic Oregon City History Resources
http://www.historicoregoncity.org/HOC/index.php?option=com_content&view=section&id=21&ltemid=75
See historical maps of Oregon and the Oregon Trail in the 1800s, and read articles about pioneer families and their travels on the Oregon Trail.

Landau, Elaine. *The Oregon Trail*. New York: Children's Press, 2006. This book outlines the basic highlights and hardships of life on the Oregon Trail.

McNeese, Tim. *The Oregon Trail: Pathway to the West*. New York: Chelsea House, 2009. Follow the stories of individual travelers on the Oregon Trail.

Oregon-California Trails Association
http://www.octa-trails.org/
Explore the history of Americans' movement west—from American Indians to settlers in prairie schooners—through detailed articles, primary sources, and more.

Oregon National Historic Trail
http://www.nps.gov/oreg/index.htm
Website visitors can plan visits to National Park Service sites on the historic Oregon Trail as well as learn about the history of the trail.

The Oregon Trail
http://www.isu.edu/~trinmich/Oregontrail.html
Read primary sources and fun facts about trail life, and explore sites that emigrants passed on the Oregon Trail.

Sutcliffe, Jane. *Sacagawea*. Minneapolis: Lerner Publications Company, 2009. Find out how Sacagawea became part of Lewis and Clark's expedition and how she was crucial to its success.

Expand learning beyond the printed book. Download free crossword puzzles, timelines, and additional website links for this book from our website, www.lerneresource.com.

Index

Photo Acknowledgments

The images in this book are used with the permission of: © iStockphoto.com/DNY59, p. 1; © iStockphoto.com/David Gomez, pp. 1 (background) and all grass backgrounds; © iStockphoto.com/sx70, pp. 3 (top), 7 (left), 9 (top) 11 (right), 16 (top), 21 (top), 26 (top), 28 (left), 33 (left), 34 (top), 37 (left), 39 (top); © iStockphoto.com/Ayse Nazli Deliormanli, pp. 3 (bottom), 43 (bottom left); © iStockphoto.com/Serdar Yagci, pp. 4-5 (background), 43 (background); © iStockphoto.com/Andrey Pustovoy, pp. 4, 17 (top), 37 (right); © North Wind Picture Archives, pp. 4 (inset), 12, 13, 14, 25, 29 (top), 32, 36, 45; © Bill Hauser & Laura Westlund/Independent Picture Service, pp. 4-5, 23, 24 (inset), 31, 38; The Denver Public Library, Western History Collection, William Henry Jackson, WHJ-10628, p. 5; © MPI/Archive Photos/Getty Images, pp. 6, 26 (bottom), 27; © Hulton Archive/Getty Images, p. 7 (right); © Peter Newark American Pictures/The Bridgeman Art Library, pp. 10, 11 (left), 44; The Denver Public Library, Western History Collection, William Henry Jackson, WHJ-10644, p. 15; The Granger Collection, New York, pp. 16 (bottom), 19; Library of Congress, pp. 17 (inset, LC-USZ62-113753), 40 (LC-USZ62-75502); © Fotosearch/Archive Photos/Getty Images, p. 18; © National Archives/Time & Life Pictures/Getty Images, p. 20; © SuperStock/SuperStock, p. 22; © iStockphoto.com/Talshiar, p. 24 (top); © Phil Schermeister/National Geographic/Getty Images, p. 24 (bottom); © ABN Images/Alamy, p. 28 (right); © Image Asset Management Ltd./SuperStock, p. 30; © Richard Cummins/Design Pics Inc. - RM Content/Alamy, p. 33 (right); © Christie's Images/SuperStock, p. 34 (bottom); © Huntington Library/SuperStock, p. 35 (top); © Science and Society/SuperStock, p. 37 (inset); © Andrew Joseph Russell/MPI/Archive Photos/Getty Images, p. 39 (bottom); The Denver Public Library, Western History Collection, J. G. Masters, Z-1957, p. 41 (top); The Art Archive/Gift of Ruth Koerner Oliver/Buffalo Bill Historical Center, Cody, Wyoming/6921.1, p. 43 (bottom middle).

Front cover: © MPI/Archive Photos/Getty Images. Back cover: © iStockphoto.com/David Gomez.

Main body text set in Sassoon Sans Regular 13.5/20. Typeface provided by Monotype Typography.